re:action

G000136886

More than fine words

does my faith impact 24/7?

Kate Hayes

MORE THAN FINE WORDS

Published by Scripture Union, 207–209 Queensway, Bletchley, MK2 2EB, England.
Email: info@scriptureunion.org.uk
Internet: www.scriptureunion.org.uk

Scripture Union Australia
Locked Bag 2, Central Coast Business Centre, NSW 2252
Website: www.su.org.au

Scripture Union USA
PO Box 987, Valley Forge, PA 19482
www.scriptureunion.org

First published 2003

ISBN 1 85999 770 8

Scripture taken from the New Living Translation, British text, published by Tyndale House Publishers, Inc, Wheaton, Illinois, USA, and distributed by STL Ltd, Carlisle, Cumbria, England; and from *The Message* © Eugene H Peterson, used by permission of NavPress Publishing Group.

British Library Cataloguing-in-Publication Data: a catalogue record for this book is available from the British Library.

Cover design and photography by David Lund Design, Milton Keynes.

Printed and bound in Great Britain by Ebenezer Baylis & Son Ltd, The Trinity Press, London Road, Worcester WR5 2JH.

Scripture Union: We are an international Christian charity working with churches in more than 130 countries providing resources to bring the good news about Jesus Christ to children, young people and families – and to encourage them to develop spiritually through the Bible and prayer. As well as our network of volunteers, staff and associates who run holidays, church-based events and school Christian groups, we produce a wide range of publications and support those who use our resources through training programmes.

Contents

Welcome!

Welcome to **re:action** discussion guides for small groups!

What are the distinctives of re:action? The series is strong on links into the contemporary world and concerned that God's Word impacts our everyday lives in practical ways. Understanding the truth leads to a response in the heart and mind of the individual. The sessions encourage personal discovery through actively exploring the Bible but, unlike many group Bible studies on the market, re:action assumes little if any prior Bible knowledge. As such it is excellent for those new to looking at Christianity, but that is not to say that the series is lightweight or lacking in depth. More mature Christians will find the series refreshing. The quality of questions should produce lively and thinking debate, and opportunities to share personal experiences. Though some humour is used, especially in the icebreaker **set the scene** sections, the content of the sessions overall is demanding and personally challenging.

Kate Hayes began writing the series out of a sense of frustration with existing materials, and everything she produces has been tried and tested in her own church groups. She says: 'Most study notes are frankly boring. Too many work on a *the answer must be Jesus* principle, regurgitating bits of text for answers. Others don't seem to relate the learning so as to make a difference to people's everyday lives. I don't write these notes because I want people to find answers to academic questions or clock up the books they've studied and then move on to something else, but because I want to see people grow in understanding and maturity. I want them to find out things that will make a difference every day of their lives, when work is tough, when friends let them down, their lives fall apart and they're faced with living as a Christian in our postmodern society.'

Each title in the series contains material for seven sessions. **Intro** gives an overview of the topic and is useful background to discussion, referred to during different sessions. **Preview** is a short introductory session that ideally would take place in a social setting, perhaps following a potluck supper or around desserts and coffee. Each session begins with **set the scene**, a light discussion opener, sometimes in the form of a quiz or game, or some fun questions. The **explore** section takes the group into the Bible text, while the **reflect** section moves into the area of personal application. Note that while most of the questions are for group discussion, there are also periods of quiet for tackling personal questions, which don't have to be shared more widely. In the closing re:action section there is opportunity to pray through what's been discussed and discovered, and sometimes suggestions for other actions both within and outside the group times.

What about leadership of the group? The re:action series is aimed at thinking people willing to be pro-active in searching the Scriptures and discussing their implications. As such, the leadership of the group, by one or two members, can be run with a light touch. The role of the re:action group leader is that of a guide through the discussion material rather than a teacher. The leader will sensitively encourage the sharing of answers and personal experiences at an appropriate level. Many questions need just one word answers and can be moved through quite quickly; at other times some brainstorming of ideas would be an appropriate response to the questions; sometimes it will be a more measured and thoughtful discussion. The leader will need to make decisions about when tangents to the discussion are legitimate and when they distract.

Ideally everyone should have their own copy of the booklet and follow through the material together. It's essential for everyone to bring a Bible, as much of the time will be spent around open Bibles. Any translation is fine, and it's often useful to compare different versions. For those new to Bible study, several contemporary translations are to be recommended: the Good News Bible, the Contemporary English Version, or the New Living Translation – and it's the NLT which is used in the booklet whenever Bible text is quoted. It will be useful to have a supply of pens, paper and perhaps card available. The sessions need little preparation. But leaders need to look ahead week by week. Sometimes scissors, newspapers and magazines are needed, for example, or photos; sometimes it might be useful to arrange furniture differently.

About the author

Kate Hayes, born into a non-churchgoing family in Sheffield, decided to become a Christian aged 12 after being 'dragged along' to a Pathfinder meeting by a friend. After studying Psychology she did teacher training but then found herself working in bookshops and in software testing for the book trade. In 1994 she moved to Dukinfield in Greater Manchester, where she now coordinates and writes materials for small groups in St John's Church.

Intro

When Christian believers gather in churches, everything that can go wrong sooner or later does. Outsiders, observing this, conclude that there is nothing to the religion business except, perhaps, business – and dishonest business at that.

Those are the words of Eugene H Peterson in the introduction to his paraphrase of the book of James in *The Message*.

The charge of hypocrisy is one frequently thrown at Christians. Many non-believers have the impression that Christians are all talk and little action; that they're free with fine words, but don't follow through.

To show the real Jesus to others, we need to be people of integrity, people who 'walk the talk', who are seen to live out in reality what we say we believe in our hearts.

James' New Testament letter is a great counter-attack on lack of depth and reality in the Church. It's addressed to Christians who were sliding off course. He writes about everyday situations, describing the ways faith in Jesus should make a visible difference in life. His message is easy to gloss over. It's easy to believe that the imperfections he discusses apply to others, not to us. As you read James and enter into the group discussions and prayer times, be open to hear God speak about the details of your life. Be prepared to be challenged, helped and encouraged to live life God's way – a life that makes a real difference because it's a life lived sincerely following Jesus.

MORE THAN FINE WORDS will encourage a small group to explore the importance of a daily life that fully reflects a commitment to Christ – through Bible-focused interaction, discussion and prayer together.

In brief

The **author** of the book of James does not introduce himself as one of the apostles, and so is unlikely to have been James, one of the original disciples. Most scholars believe that he was one of the key leaders of the Jewish Christians in Jerusalem, and a half-brother of Jesus.

It is thought that this letter was one of the first books of the New Testament to be written, possibly before AD 50. Others date it later, but as James was almost certainly martyred in the early 60s, that would mean AD 61 or 62.

Why did he write it? After early Christian leader Stephen was martyred by stoning, the persecution of the early Christians led to them scattering away from Jerusalem. James wrote to encourage them in their faith in the face of difficult times.

1 Preview

And remember, it is a message to obey, not just to listen to.
If you don't obey, you are only fooling yourself.

James 1:22

set the scene

Brands are everywhere; cool and trendy, sedate and expensive, cheap and nasty. We're supposed to be able to tell a great deal about a person by the brands they choose to buy and use – or is that just an urban myth?

Divide into groups of three or four, with each group choosing one or two of the following brands:

Nike
Your local supermarket's 'value' range
Volvo
Cafedirect
The Sun Newspaper
Harley-Davidson
Rolex
Pot Noodle

Q: What image do you have of a 'typical' person who buys and uses this brand? (For example, their age, appearance, job, personality and interests.)

Q: Why do you think they choose this brand over another?

Alternatively Another way of tackling this activity is to take along a pile of magazines. Cut out pictures of brand name goods and pictures of the kinds of people that might use these items. Make a collage poster and talk through your ideas with the rest of the small groups.

For each brand you've chosen, consider these questions:

Q: If Christianity was a brand, what image might a non-Christian have of a typical Christian?

Q: What elements of this description do you think are generally fair?

Q: What elements would you challenge?

During 2001 Marks and Spencer suffered a temporary but widely publicised decline in their sales. Confidence in their clothing had plummeted. Yet, not many years previously, it had occupied a prime position on the nation's high streets, seen as the 'best of British', and at its peak sold a third of all women's underwear.

Q: Has your underwear drawer ever contained M&S products?

Q: Why?

Q: What do you think causes a popular retailer to suffer such a decline in sales?

Reality check The reputation of a brand is crucial, influencing its target audience, its sales and ultimately its survival. It doesn't matter how well known a name is; its products must live up to expectations.

Christianity isn't a brand and we are called to meet God's expectations – not anybody else's. However, most people are going to form their opinions of Jesus through their contact with Christians. We are his living advertisements and our reputation matters.

Sometimes people will find a mismatch between their expectation of what Christians are like and the reality.

- If those expectations are built on long-ago experiences of dull churches and out-of-touch Christians, then we may be able to challenge and change them and be glad to do so.
- If those expectations are built on experiences of Christians who say one thing and do another, then we have a problem. Many

people dismiss Christianity and Jesus because they don't see a positive difference in the way Christians live.

Read

Luke 10:27

Q: How are we called to live?

It sounds very simple but we know it isn't!

Read

Romans 7:15

Q: Have you experienced something of the internal battle Paul describes here? In pairs, share how much or how little you identify with him.

explore

Read

Luke 18:10–14

Q: How would you sum up the public image of the Pharisees? The tax collectors?

Q: Why did Jesus commend the tax collector and not the Pharisee?

Q: What warning does this passage offer us?

reflect

Read through the **Intro** and reflect for a few minutes on your own on the kind of person you are. Are you naturally resistant to change? Or open to the possibility of doing things differently? Do you prefer to do things your own way? Or are you willing to consider other approaches?

re:action

Ask one person to **read** out the lines from Psalm 139:23,24 (in bold) below and someone else to **read** the interwoven prayer. Allow a short time of **silence** between each section.

Search me, O God, and know my heart; test me and know my thoughts.

> Lord, you know everything there is to know about me.
> Help me to trust myself to you completely.
> Teach me to be honest with you.

Point out anything in me that offends you,

> Show me the things in my life that I need to change.
> Where my words and actions don't match up,
> Where I need to become more like Jesus.
> Forgive me for my past mistakes and allow me a new start.

And lead me along the path of everlasting life.

> I choose to follow you forever.
> Give me the strength to serve you wholeheartedly.
> Thank you that you are with me all the way.

If your group is confident with open prayer, you could ask them to **pray** in response to each verse or section.

Then **pray** that God will speak to each person in the group as you study James together. **Ask** him to show you things in your lives that need to change, and for grace to work at that challenge.

This coming week It will be really helpful to read right through the book of James before the next session. Try a contemporary version such as the *New International Version*, the *New Living Translation* or the *Contemporary English Version*; or an imaginative paraphrase like *The Message*.

2 Ready for anything

For when your faith is tested, your endurance has a chance to grow. So let it grow, for when your endurance is fully developed, you will be strong in character and ready for anything.

James 1:3,4

set the scene

For each of the four questions choose your response from the eight listed:

Q: If the electricity was cut off halfway through cooking a posh meal for your family or friends?

My response would be No: ___

Q: If the builders knocked down the wrong wall?

My response would be No: ___

Q: If you ran over your neighbour's adored cat?

My response would be No: ___

Q: If your boss irrevocably deleted your last month's work from the computer?

My response would be No: ___

Responses:

1 scream and shout
2 run away
3 cry
4 blame someone else… who?
5 start again
6 hide the evidence
7 change my plans… to what?
8 something else… what?

Alternatively Your group may enjoy this activity more. Split into smaller groups. Ask each group to choose one of the situations and put together a short drama showing how different people might react to the same disaster. Perform for the others, and then discuss how the group members would have reacted in that situation and why.

Q: What is your worst experience of a disaster like these?

Q: How did you react then?

explore

Next we're going to look at whether being a Christian makes a difference to the way we deal with difficulty or trouble.

1 Experiencing joy in troubles

Read

James 1:1–4,12

Q: What might James mean here by *trouble* or *trials*?

Q: How does he say we should respond to tough times?

Q: How do you react to James' statement?

Q: Why should we have joy in these experiences?

Reality check Joy – which James says we should experience – is not the same as happiness. Happiness is based on our current circumstances. If we're in pain, tired, lonely, late for work, wet, cold and hungry … we're not likely to feel happy. However, we can still be joyful because joy is based on the unchanging reality of God's promises to us and his presence in our lives.

Read

1 Peter 1:8,9
Romans 8:28

Q: What extra insights do these verses give you about joy?

Our call We have a choice about how we respond to a tough situation. James says, 'So **let** it grow... ' (verse 4). In other words, we **choose** to let God in or push him out, he won't force his will upon us.

Q: Can you think of a time when you, or someone you know, faced this kind of choice in a difficult situation?

Q: Which choice did you (or they) make?

Q: How did it work out in the end?

This is where being a Christian should make a difference. It doesn't protect us from meeting tough situations and testing times. It doesn't protect us from feeling pain or anger or grief. But it should make a difference in the way we respond. It should mean we allow God into the situation.

Q: How do we allow God into these tough situations? What do we have to do?

Q: What good things come from sharing our bad times with God?

Reality check What James is talking about is more than just survival. It's about learning to take the longer view. It's about celebrating the good that bad times can produce in us. Paul says, 'You ... must run in such a way that you will win. All athletes practise strict self-control. They do it to win a prize that will fade away, but we do it for an eternal prize' (1 Corinthians 9:24b,25).

2 Becoming mature Christians

Read

James 1:5–8,16–19

Q: As we endure, our maturity grows (1:4). How do we find out what to do with this newly-acquired maturity?

Q: Are you able to ask God for wisdom confidently, as James suggests?

Q: What makes this possible or impossible for you?

Q: In *The Message*, these verses say: *Ask boldly, believingly, without a second thought. People who 'worry their prayers' are like wind-whipped waves. Don't think you're going to get anything from the Master that way, adrift at sea, keeping all your options open.* What does it mean to 'keep our options open' when we pray?

Q: Why might such an attitude mean that we can't receive anything from God? Does keeping our options open work against wholehearted trust in God? Are our decisions based on fluctuating emotions? Or determined confidence in God expressed in action?

Q: Is it possible for someone to be a 'real' Christian and still have doubts? If we have doubts, how can we cope? Check out Mark 9:24.

3 Trusting in God

Read
James 1:13–18

We base this trust in God on:

- God's character
- our relationship with him

re:action

Q: From these verses, what is God like?

Q: What does he think of us?

reflect

Q: What are you finding tough going in your life at the moment? Think about one area in particular.

Q: Have you decided to trust God in this area? Or are you still 'keeping your options open'?

Q: How is being a Christian making a difference to you in this concern?

Q: Is there anything you need to change in the way you are responding to this situation?

Q: How could you begin to do that?

Q: How could the other members of your group pray for you in this situation?

re:action

Praise God for things in his character that you really appreciate. **Share** Bible verses that describe an element of God's character such as his power, love or holiness. **Sing or listen** to a recording of a song or hymn that talks about what God is like

Pray together. If your group is not very confident praying aloud then begin by spending a few minutes **talking** about God's character together, **making a list** of ideas as you go along. When you pray, go round the group with each person saying, 'Lord, I praise you that you are … ' then naming one of the things from the list. Don't worry if some things are mentioned by more than one person in the group.

Pray for one another. Those who are willing could **share** some of the things they thought about in the `Reflect` section. Or one person could say each member's name in turn, followed by a short silence during which the group can quietly pray, then move onto the next name.

Close by **reading together** James 1:17,18:

Whatever is good and perfect comes to us from God above, who created all heaven's lights. Unlike them, he never changes or casts shifting shadows. In his goodness he chose to make us his own children by giving us his true word. And we, out of all creation, became his choice possession.

3 Pride and prejudice

*Yes indeed, it is good when you truly obey our Lord's royal command
found in the Scriptures: 'Love your neighbour as yourself.'*

James 2:8

set the scene

Making links Give out copies of everyone's names on sheets of paper
with plenty of space alongside each name. Each person has to find out
at least one thing they have in common with each other member of the
group, writing it next to that person's name.

What's allowed? Well, you might find someone else in the group who,
like you:

- has a pink bathroom suite
- likes jazz
- had chicken jalfrezi for supper
- has been for a trip in a hot air balloon
- studied engineering at college
- wears purple slippers

The more obscure the link you can find the better. Both being women
or both having ten toes? That's too feeble to count! And you must find
a different link to each member of your group – no repeats.

Then what? When everyone has finished, given up, or time's run out,
sit down and go round the group. Each person describes the link they
found with the next person on their left. When you've finished, go back
round the group again the other way, this time stating your link with
the person on your right. You might like to award a chocolate biscuit
for the most creative or obscure links!

explore

This part of the session will look at discrimination/favouritism in the

Church. Does it exist? Should it? How should being a Christian make a difference to the way I treat people?

1 Discrimination in the Church

Read

James 2:1–4

Q: Two newcomers arrive at a church meeting. The Welcome Team zoom into action, directing them to a seat. But where do these men end up?

Q: Why are they treated so differently to each other?

Q: How do you think the two men felt about their visit to the church? Describe how the rich man felt. And the poor man?

Read

James 2:5–7

Q: Why does James say the treatment of the rich man was particularly foolish?

Q: We're part of a world where some people are valued more highly than others – and for all kinds of reasons. What kind of people does our society admire? Why?

Q: What kind of people does our society neglect or overlook?

Reality check Attitudes that are common in society can influence our behaviour. Sometimes we don't even notice these attitudes, far less challenge them. The Church has often encouraged discrimination and division instead of standing up against such evils. James says (1:27) that we must 'refuse to let the world corrupt us'. Unintentional discrimination is no better for those on the receiving end than deliberate prejudice; James reminds us that our faith should make a real difference to the way we treat others.

Read

1 John 3:1
Galatians 3:28
Romans 12:4,5

Q: So, how should we view other people?

Read

Romans 15:7
Philippians 2:2–7
1 Peter 3:8,9

Q: And how should we behave towards one another?

2 The consequences of favouritism

Read

James 2:8–13

Q: How does James describe those who show favouritism?

Q: What warning does he give?

Q: What difference do you think it would make if the Church lived out God's call to value everyone equally? Why?

reflect

We may not be impressed by the welcoming techniques of the early Christians but how can we be sure prejudice doesn't exist in our church too in some forms? Our claims to welcome and include everyone equally will not be reflected in practice, and it won't be those of us who feel at home and secure who are most likely to notice.

Our strengths Who will probably come into our church and feel welcome and at home 'with people like me'? Please note: this is not the same as who we *think* is welcome in our church. Before you answer this question consider:

- What groups of people are well represented? Think about factors such as people's age, gender, race, health, education, employment, housing...
- Who takes part in services, other events and groups?
- What assumptions underlie the way we do things? For example: How would someone cope in our church if they couldn't read? What about money, mobility, family links?

And weaknesses If those are our strengths, who might be feeling 'one on my own' and marginalised in our church? Feeling different is often compounded by our needs or values being overlooked by others.

Q: Why does this happen – unintentionally or not?

Q: What could our church do to correct this?

Q: What could I do?

Q: Is there someone you need to treat differently in future? What will you do?

re:action

Begin by **thinking** about being sorry. **Focus** on any intentional or accidental favouring of one group over another. Have one person **read** the words of 1 John 1:8–10 and then **say a prayer** together – either one - you use in confession at your church; or you could compose one sentence prayers and read them out around the group; or you could pray around the group.

Next, think about **saying thank you**. Spend a few minutes in silence, thinking of those people who make you feel valued. Think about what it is they do that makes such a difference to you. As you continue in silence, thank God for these people and all they give to you. Perhaps you could decide to send them a card this week, telling them how much you appreciate them.

Finally, **look outwards**. One person could **read** 1 Corinthians 13:4–7 as the others listen.

This version is *The Message*, but choose whichever your group would prefer.

Love never gives up.
  Love cares more for others than for self.
Love doesn't want what it doesn't have.
  Love doesn't strut,
Doesn't have a swelled head,
  Doesn't force itself on others,
Isn't always 'me first',
  Doesn't fly off the handle,
Doesn't keep score of the sins of others,
  Doesn't revel when others grovel,
Takes pleasure in the flowering of truth,
  Puts up with anything,
Trusts God always,
  Always looks for the best,
Never looks back,
  But keeps going to the end.

Pray that God would help you to care for others in this way.

4 Proof of the pudding

Dear brothers and sisters, what's the use of saying you have faith if you don't prove it by your actions? That kind of faith can't save anyone.

James 2:14

set the scene

Start with one person slowly reading out a list of 20 small household items, repeating it until one minute is up. No one else should be able to see the list. At the end of the time give people two minutes to write down as many of the items as they can remember.

Then repeat the game in its more traditional form. Put 20 small items on a tray. Don't use any of the items on the list you just read out. Again, give people one minute to look at the items without touching them, then take them away. Allow everyone two minutes to write down as many items as they can remember.

Read out the correct answers and see how many people have remembered.

Q: What techniques did people use to remember the items?

Q: Did people do better at the first or second version of the game?

Q: Why do you think that was?

explore

Looking at some verses in James, we're going to consider whether faith makes a difference to behaviour.

1 Listen and obey

Read

James 1:22–25; 2:14–26

Q: How would you sum up what James is saying in these two passages?

Try this You might like to give people a few minutes to come up with a snappy slogan based on James' message here. Your group could memorise it or write in on a mini poster as a reminder through the week.

Slogan:

2 Fitting faith and good actions together

Read

James 2:24
Romans 4:5

Q: What do we learn from these verses about a) the relationship between faith and good actions and b) their importance?

Case study: Dougal and Dylan

Dougal describes himself as a Christian. Goes to church on Sundays and home group midweek. Friendly and polite. Knows his Bible well. Happily discusses Christian things with the interested at work, home, church or in his social life. BUT… not your man if you need something. Quotes 'helpful' verses and makes vague suggestions of calling round or helping out but doesn't carry them out. Especially shy of anything that might involve more than a one-off commitment. Not free with his time or his possessions.

Dylan never sets foot in church. Not at all sure whether he believes in God. Certainly wouldn't say he was a Christian. BUT… helps anyone with anything. Puts himself out – without expecting anything back. Generous and kind. Gives with a smile. Always ready to go the extra mile.

Q: Can you recognise either Dougal or Dylan from verses we've read from James 2?

Reality check It's a puzzle! Some Christians seem to care for no one other than themselves; they do nothing much for anyone. In contrast, some non-Christians live lives of sacrificial care and love for others. Perhaps you know people like Dougal and Dylan. Perhaps you can see yourself in one of them.

Q: Dylan lives a life full of good deeds and love for others. Why isn't it enough to put him right with God? What is enough?

Read
Romans 3:20, 22–28
Galatians 2:16

Q: So where do James' comments about good deeds fit in?

Read again
James 2:21–24

Q: Can you think of anything that Jesus said that would help our understanding here?

Read
Luke 11:28
Matthew 28:20

Think it through Do you think Paul and James agree or disagree about faith and actions? Paul says that faith is all we need to be put right with God but James reminds us that words are easy to say. As Christians our lives have to show we mean what we say. The only things that prove we have faith are our actions, our good deeds, the way we live.

re:action

Read

1 John 3:18,19

Q: Is there someone you need to show your love to?

Q: What does James say about the faith of those who don't put what they hear into practice?

in 1:22

in 2:14

in 2:17

in 2:20

in 2:26

Read

1 Timothy 5:25
Matthew 7:1–5
1 Corinthians 4:5

Q: What are we warned against in these verses?

reflect

Q: We hear so many messages… in sermons, books, Bible notes, group studies… it would be impossible to act on all of them at once, wouldn't it? How can we decide which things to act on and which to leave for now?

Q: Think back to anything you read or heard in the last few weeks that struck you as being important. Can you recall it?

Q: Do you measure the effectiveness of any message by how enjoyable it was? How solidly based on the Bible? How much you allowed it to impact your life?

Q: Do you have any suggestions for turning listening into action? Hebrews 10:24 offers one starting point. Can you think of others?

re:action

Give everyone a piece of paper or thin card. **Draw** round your hand and cut out the shape. On one side of your hand shape **write** either the slogan you came up with earlier, or choose a verse that you feel sums up James' message.

Hands can be used to put thought into action. **Sit quietly** together, looking at the message written on your hand shape and **reflect** on some of the things God has wanted you to learn lately. What changes does he want you to make, what actions to take?

If something comes into your mind, **write** it on the reverse side of your hand shape. Only **show** or **share** it with the others in the group if you want to. If you don't think of anything at the moment, keep the hand and when God does speak to you, make a note of it then. Pray for one another, aloud or in silence, particularly anyone facing the challenge of change.

5 Sticks and stones

Dear friends, be quick to listen, slow to speak, and slow to get angry.

James 1:19

set the scene

Q: Flimflam... Mermaid... Rapprochement... Chinook... Have you got a favourite word? Something that you enjoy because of its meaning? Or the way it sounds? Or a strong association with a person, a wonderful memory or an exceptional experience? Share any of your favourite words or phrases with the rest of the group.

Q: Do you have a 'catch phrase' ... something you say often, and which others might associate with you?

Alternatively... your group might like to try this. Give everyone a piece of paper with the name of a different emotion on it. You could use words like:

anger	sadness	joy	triumph
despair	boredom	frustration	disappointment
curiosity	fear	confusion	disgust

Then decide on a simple sentence such as:

- The bus is coming.
- That's my egg.
- It's housegroup tonight.

Each person in turn says the sentence trying to express the emotion on their piece of paper. The rest of the group have to guess their emotion.

explore

Having looked at whether faith should make a difference to what we *do*, we're now going to consider the impact of faith on what we *say*.

1 Two ears, one mouth

Read

James 1:19,20

Q: Are you quicker to listen or to speak?

Q: When we speak, what can we learn about someone who is listening to us?

Q: When we listen, what can we learn about someone who is speaking to us?

Q: When we *really* listen, we can find out more than words alone can tell us. Why do you think this kind of listening is often difficult?

Q: What do we give to someone by making the time and effort to listen to them properly?

Q: How might listening to someone help us to be slow to get angry with them? But when might anger be justified?

Q: If our anger is justified, does that mean we can express it any way we want?

2 Controlling the fire

Read

James 3:1–12

Q: Why should we aim to control our tongue?

Share around the group the verses below, from Proverbs. This book has a great deal to say about the way we speak to one another. Make a list together of the kinds of speech we should avoid and why.

Verse	wrong ways to speak	because it leads to...
11:9		
15:1		
15:4		
16:28		
17:9		
17:19		
25:18		

Q: What other kinds of speech do we need to avoid?

Q: How does James sum up the negative effects of the wrong kind of speech? (Check out James 3:6.)

If these are the things to avoid, what should we be aiming for instead? Look at this second list of verses from Proverbs. Use them to make a list of good ways to speak to one another and the benefits that brings. Once you've finished the list, you might like to write it out on a piece of card to make a bookmark or a group poster and use it as a reminder.

Verse	right ways to speak	because it leads to...
12:18		
15:4		
16:24		
21:23		
24:26		
25:15		
27:9		

Q: How do you feel when someone speaks to you in one of these good ways?

Q: Why do you think the way we speak to people matters so much to them?

3 Keeping on track

Read

Matthew 12:34; 15:18,19
Luke 6:45

Q: What does the way we speak reveal about us?

Q: So how do we keep our tongue from causing big damage? Check out the following verses and share your thoughts.

Read

James 3:2
2 Peter 1:6
Colossians 3:8–11
Galatians 5:22–25

reflect

Q: 'Quick to listen, slow to speak, slow to get angry'. Which of these are you best at?

Q: Which do you need to work on most?

Q: Think about those closest to you. Would they agree with your assessment?

Q: What could you do to start working on this area this week? Look back again at James 1:22 as you consider your answer.

Q: Think about your friends, your family, your colleagues and your neighbours. What characterises the way you generally speak to them?

Q: Are there ways you could improve on this?

Q: What benefits might that change bring to you? And to them?

re:action

God is never too busy to listen to us. **Read together** Psalm 17:6:

> *I am praying to you because I know you will answer, O God.*
> *Bend down and listen as I pray.*

And Isaiah 59:1:

> *Listen! The Lord is not too weak to save you,*
> *and he is not becoming deaf.*
> *He can hear you when you call.*

Give thanks for the way God is always willing to listen to anything we want to say to him. What do you want to say to him at the moment? Spend some time **sharing** what is on your heart with him. You could do this through writing, silent prayer or praying aloud. Perhaps you could pray in turn around the group, and if someone doesn't want to **pray** aloud, they could pray in silence and then touch the next person on the arm to show they have finished.

End by spending a few minutes **listening** for God to speak to you. You could begin this by listening to a song or other piece of music to help you **focus** your mind on God. Give people a chance to share anything they felt God say to them if they wish to.

6 When Christians fall out

Don't speak evil against each other, my dear brothers and sisters.

James 4:11a

set the scene

Q: How do you normally cope with conflict? Do you:

- Respond angrily – 'I'll show them...'
- Run away and hide – 'If they can't find me, they can't hurt me (and I can't hurt them!)'
- Ignore it and hope it goes away – 'Problem, what problem?'
- Do something else? What?

Q: Think of a time when you, or someone you know, reacted to conflict in one of these ways. Did it solve things?

Q: What problems can be caused when someone:

- responds angrily?
- runs away?
- ignores the problem?

Q: How do you feel when you are in conflict with someone?

explore

For this section we're going to turn our attention to how our faith might make a difference to dealing with conflict.

Read

1 John 3:11
1 Corinthians13:4,5
Ephesians 2:16
Colossians 3:15

Q: From these verses, what would you say our life together should be like?

Read

James 4:1–6,11,12

Q: However much we know the Church should be people loving one another and reflecting Jesus to one another, the reality often falls short and relationships deteriorate. What reasons does James give for this?

Q: Do you think his comments are fair?

Q: What happens to a relationship if conflict blows over, but the underlying issues remain unresolved?

Reality check It's uncompromising! As Christians we are called to live together as one people. We are the body of Christ. We are expected not just to sort out the immediate problem – but to live in restored, harmonious relationships as well.

Dealing with conflict

1 Is it me? Am I in the wrong?

Read

Galatians 5:6–23

Q: What kind of wrong motives and attitudes can lead to conflict?

Q: What attitudes would help us in sorting out conflict? And what attitudes are counter-productive?

2 Is it really important?

Read

Colossians 3:13
Ephesians 4:2

Q: What do these verses suggest we should do whenever possible?

Q: How can we decide when to let something drop and when to pursue it?

Q: Of course, there is nothing wrong with disagreeing with someone as such – but the way we do it can cause problems. How do we live alongside people with very different views to our own?

Risk it to fix it We cannot know for certain how someone will respond to our approach. In attempting to put things right we risk the other person refusing to cooperate, retaliating, even deciding to end the relationship. However, we are expected to give it our best shot. How do we go about it?

Step 1 – Take the initiative: Matthew 5:24

Q: It's easy enough to see that we should take the first step if we are the one in the wrong but what if we really don't think we are? Why should we still take the first step when it's not our fault?

Q: What would be a good way to start the conversation in this situation?

Step 2 – Do it soon: Matthew 5:25

Q: We're unlikely to end up in jail when we don't sort out our disagreements with one another, but this advice still applies. What can happen to a relationship if you don't sort things out quickly?

Step 3 – Be honest: Ephesians 4:25

Q: Why is it often hard to be truthful with someone in this kind of situation?

Q: What are the benefits of honesty?

Q: How do we balance the need for honesty with the need for love? Check out Ephesians 4:15. Total honesty can sometimes be felt as harsh.

The result

Read
Matthew 18:15–22

Q: What are the two possible results of tackling conflict?

Q: What should we do if our first attempt doesn't work out? And if it's successful?

Q: Should we forgive someone who isn't sorry? Why/why not?

Q: Are there risks in forgiving someone?

Q: Is it possible to trust someone who has hurt us in the past?

Q: What good things come when we sort out conflicts successfully?

3 Reducing the risk of conflict

Read

James 3:17,18

Q: What qualities does James describe as the marks of a wise person?

Q: What benefits come to those who live like this?

Q: Which of these do you think you are best at?

Q: And which do you need to develop most?

Read

James 4:7–10

Q: How do these verses help us as we think about dealing with and reducing conflict in our lives?

reflect

Q: Would you describe yourself as an argumentative person or a peacemaker?

Q: Do you think your friends, family and colleagues would agree with you?

Spend a few minutes in quiet. Are you in conflict with someone at the moment? How would you describe the problem in a sentence or two? What does your description reveal about your motives and attitudes? How are you going to start sorting out that relationship? Could the rest of your group pray for you?

For later... If you would find it helpful, why not write a letter to the person you are in conflict with this week and give it to them. As we write a letter, we have time to think about what we're going to say. As the other person reads the letter, they take time to reflect before they have to respond. Remember to affirm good things in your relationship with the person. Try not to be too negative. Avoid email if you can – comments can seem more abrupt than you meant.

re:action

Begin by **reflecting** quietly on the times you have been involved in conflict with others, especially if it is a problem for you at the moment. If appropriate, give everyone a few minutes to write their own short prayer of repentance. Follow that by **reading** Psalm 51 together, or have one person read it while the others listen.

Share your prayer needs from the `Reflect` section with the rest of the group, if you'd like to. Make sure everyone understands and is willing to respect everyone's privacy by keeping information confidential. Do be wise in how much you share, especially if others in the group know the people involved. Avoiding using names or specific details will prevent prayer requests becoming gossip or causing damage to the other person's reputation with those present.

Pray for right relationships within the wider church, your group and each individual's life.

Remember, it is sin to know what you ought to do and then not do it.

James 4:17

set the scene

Answer yes or no for each question:

- I have at least one diary and I use it regularly.
- I pay my bills on time even when they're not on direct debit/ standing order.
- I know what I'm having for supper every night this week and I've bought most of it already.
- Each step in my job/career has been carefully planned out.
- I have a list when I go shopping and I use it.
- I buy my Christmas cards and presents as early as possible.
- When I do something, I have a picture of how it's going to work out before I start.
- I write/wrote homework and revision timetables and stuck to them.
- All my phone numbers, addresses etc are up to date and in a book together.

Count up your yes and no answers. Lots of yes answers might say that you are someone who plans to live: lots of no answers that you are someone whose only real plan is to take it as it comes!

Q: Do your results accurately reflect your enthusiasm (or lack of it) for planning?

Q: Why do or don't you like to plan?

Q: What good things come from living a planned life?

Q: What good things come from taking life as it comes?

explore

Is planning an area of life where we might expect our faith to have an influence?

Read

James 4:13–16

Q: So, is James saying it's wrong to make plans in life?

Q: Is it possible to live without ever making any plans?

Q: Look back at James 4:15. How literally should we take this? Why/ why not?

Q: As James reminds us, we can't assume that we know what is going to happen tomorrow, let alone have total control over our lives – however much we may want it. So, how do you feel about this?

Q: How do you cope with the uncertainty in life? And how do you think God would want us to cope with it?

Now let's turn our attention to one of the big uncertainties about life – our health.

Read

James 5:13–20

Q: How do you react when you're ill?

- It's a great excuse for chocolate, daytime TV and a day off work!
- I hibernate under the duvet with a hot water bottle.
- I play the victim and annoy everyone around me by moaning and groaning.
- I hit the chemist bigtime and dose myself up to the eyeballs.
- Me? I'm never ill!
- Other… what?

Humour aside, sickness and healing often seem one of the most complicated areas of the Christian life. We are called to pray for healing and yet so often don't see it. The good do sometimes die young.

Q: What, according to James 5:13, should we do when we are suffering in some way? What attitude to prayer is James recommending here?

Q: Sometimes when we pray it appears that nothing changes. How should we cope with this?

Q: Are you someone who can keep on praying in tough situations? Or do you give up?

Q: How can we encourage one another to go on praying through difficult times?

Case study: Wayne, Patrick and Jessica

One morning Wayne wakes up with a bit of a sniffle. Round the corner, Patrick develops a migraine over breakfast. And Jessica, a couple of streets away, has got an ear infection. Being good Christians from the local church, they start their days with their usual Bible reading notes, despite all feeling under the weather. Funnily enough, the passage for the day for all three is from James 5!

Not too far away, the vicar – having, of course, completed his usual three-hour daily prayer vigil! – is tucking into his porridge when the phone rings. And again. And again. Wayne, Patrick and Jessica have all called to request a visit from the leadership team for prayer and anointing with oil.

Q: Is this what James means? Are our three Christians being obedient to God's Word? What would you do if you were Wayne? Or the vicar?

Q: How does your church support sick people? Is this best practice? Can you think of improvements to suggest to the leadership?

Myth alert! Some churches/church leaders teach that illness or continuing illness means a lack of faith on the part of the sick person. What does James say? Whose faith brings healing, according to 5:15? But is healing 'guaranteed' anyway?

Read

2 Corinthians 12:7–9
1 Timothy 5:23
2 Timothy 4:20

Q: Who, in these verses, are ill?

Q: Who, can we assume, was praying for them?

It would be difficult to say that Paul was someone who was lacking in faith, yet clearly he and his friends were not always healed – in spite of James' assertion, *the Lord will make them well*. However, compare this experience with Acts 28:9.

Read

Matthew 9:1–8

Q: What does Jesus say first to the paralysed man?

Q: What kind of healing did Jesus bring to this man?

Q: What does James say will also happen when the elders pray (5:15)?

Reality check So, when the Bible speaks about healing it doesn't just mean *physical* healing but *spiritual* healing – being right with God – as well.

Q: How does James encourage us to put ourselves right with God?

Spend a few minutes in silence thinking about confession to others. Are you comfortable with the idea? Think about the potential benefits, and potential disadvantages.

reflect

Look at the recurring word 'remember' in these three pieces of advice from James:

> *Remember, it is sin to know what you ought to do and then not do it. (4:17)*

> *Remember, it is a message to obey, not just to listen to. If you don't obey, you are only fooling yourself. (1:22)*

> *So whenever you speak, or whatever you do, remember that you will be judged by the law of love, the law that set you free. (2:12)*

As we've looked at James and other parts of the Bible together, we've looked at how being a Christian should make a difference in the way we live. We should not be indistinguishable from those around us who don't know Jesus. In some things at least we should stand out in such a way that our lives show the light and love of Jesus.

We should be different:

- in the way we respond to trouble and sickness
- in the way we treat other people, with love and acceptance not prejudice and favouritism

- in the way we speak to and relate to one another

so that our words are reflected in our actions and our actions reflect the God who lives within us.

Here are some questions for quiet reflection on your own:

Q: What has made most impression on you as you've studied with the group?

Q: Are there good things you've found out about the way you live?

Q: Where has God pointed out ways you need to change? Have you begun to do something about it?

Q: What do you need to work on most at the moment?

re:action

Pray on your own, considering areas of your life where you haven't yet allowed God to make a difference. Ask him to help you change.

Then **give thanks** for one another, for the things God has taught you and for the time that everyone has given to learning and sharing together. One or more people could **pray** for the group.

Begin a time of **praise** with someone reading James 1:17:

Whatever is good and perfect comes to us from God above, who created all heaven's lights. Unlike them, he never changes or casts shifting shadows.

As many as would like to can give a prayer of thanks for the unchanging God who is the source of every good thing we have and is always with us. You could also choose one or two songs to **sing** together or to listen to.

Conclude with everyone **reading** Psalm 62:5–8 as a declaration of confidence in a God who is to be trusted and who wants the best for his people, a God who gives us the strength to change our thinking, speaking and behaving to reflect a faith that impacts the 24/7.

I wait quietly before God,
    for my hope is in him.
He alone is my rock and my salvation,
    my fortress where I will not be shaken.
My salvation and my honour come from God alone.
    He is my refuge, a rock where no enemy can reach me.

O my people, trust in him at all times.
    Pour out your heart to him,
        for God is our refuge.

Re:action small group Bible resources by Kate Hayes

Others in the series

For the tough times

Does God care when I'm hurting?
Whether it's thousands killed in a terrorist attack as you watch on TV, your next door neighbour on chemo for cancer, or your best friend's marriage on shaky ground … there's no escaping the issue of suffering. Maybe you want to shout at God that it's just so unfair! Just what's it all for?

ISBN 1 85999 622 1

Chosen for change

Am I part of God's big plan?
Like it or not, you're living in the 'me' culture. Are you comfortable with going it alone, taking care of 'Number One', cashing in on 'your rights' and turning a blind eye to responsibilities? What about sharing… caring… belonging… teamwork… community? Are you ready to serve not self – but society?

ISBN 1 85999 623 X

The possibility of purpose

What's the meaning of my life?
A treadmill existence of deadlines and pressures? Or a kaleidoscope of amazing opportunities? What's your take on daily life? Do you see yourself as a meaningless cosmic dust speck? Or a significant mover in a master-plan? Your view affects your motivation, your self-esteem, your priorities, your everyday choices…

ISBN 1 85999 620 5

Jesus: the sequel

Is he really coming back?
Appointments, schedules, timetables … we live in a time-bound society. It's so easy to live just for the present. Are you ready for the future? Not just your next career move… your next property… your next set of wheels… or even your plans for retirement. But the future that begins when Jesus himself returns!

ISBN 1 85999 621 3

More than bricks and ritual

Am I a team player for God? Community is under threat. Contemporary lifestyles work against building relationships. Lives are increasingly independent and isolated. What of the Church? Does your life just briefly overlap with Christians on a Sunday morning? Are you missing out on God's vision for us as brothers and sisters? As a family? As a team?

ISBN 1 85999 769 4

church@home

SU's new web magazine on the world of small groups

www.scriptureunion.org.uk/churchathome